TO MY FRIEND

THERE IS SWEET MUSIC

PART-SONG FOR S.S.A.A.T.T.B.B.

THE WORDS WRITTEN BY TENNYSON

THE MUSIC COMPOSED BY

EDWARD ELGAR.

(OP. 53, No. 1.)

* Some Contraltos should sing with the 1st Tenors.

2

Four unaccompanied Part-songs
Opus 53

for SATB with divisions

Edward Elgar

Order No. NOV072324R

NOVELLO PUBLISHING LIMITED
14-15 Berners Street, London, W1T 3LJ

CONTENTS

here that soft-er falls Than pet-als from blown ro-ses on the grass ; Mu -

here that soft-er falls Than pet-als from blown ro-ses on the grass ; . .

here that soft-er falls Than pet-als from blown ro-ses on the grass ; . .

here that soft-er falls Than pet-als from blown ro-ses on the grass ; . .

8

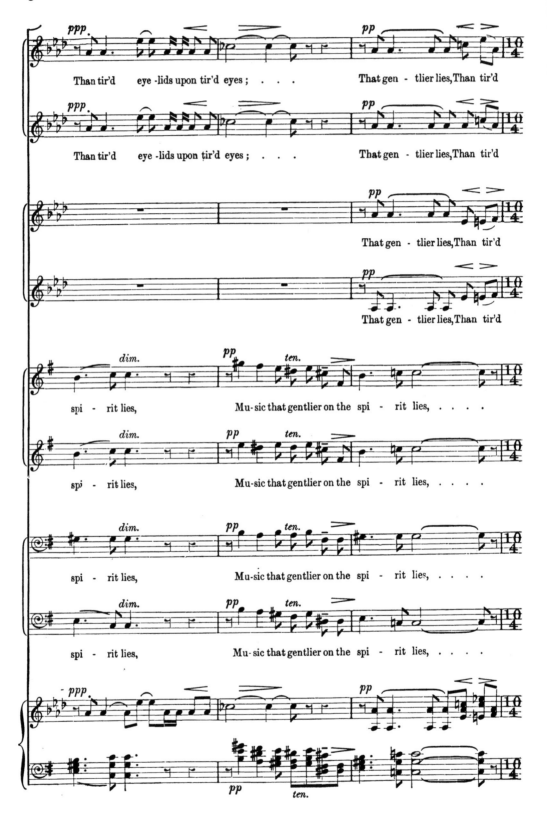

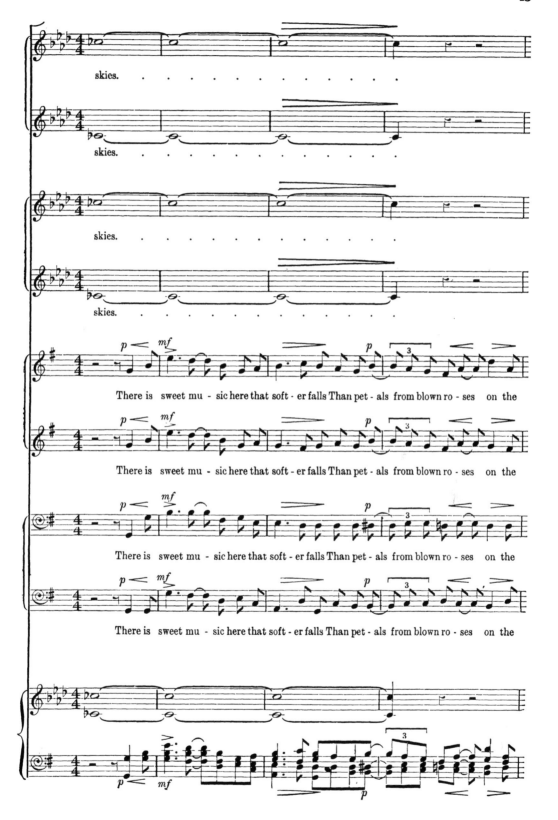

skies.

skies.

skies.

skies.

There is sweet mu - sic here that soft - er falls Than pet - als from blown ro - ses on the

There is sweet mu - sic here that soft - er falls Than pet - als from blown ro - ses on the

There is sweet mu - sic here that soft - er falls Than pet - als from blown ro - ses on the

There is sweet mu - sic here that soft - er falls Than pet - als from blown ro - ses on the

14

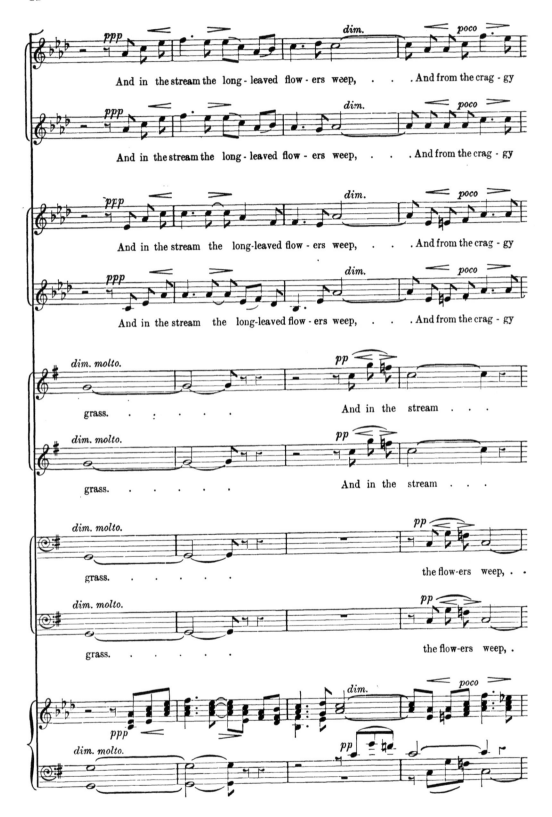

ledge the pop-py hangs in sleep, ... hangs in sleep, . . .

ledge the pop-py hangs in sleep, ... hangs in sleep, . . .

ledge the pop-py hangs in sleep, ... hangs in sleep, . .

ledge the pop-py hangs in sleep, ... hangs in sleep, . . .

And from the crag

the pop-py

And from the crag-gy ledge

the pop-py hangs,

16

Rome, Dec., 1907.

TO JULIA H. WORTHINGTON.

DEEP IN MY SOUL

PART-SONG FOR S.A.T.B.

THE WORDS WRITTEN BY BYRON

THE MUSIC COMPOSED BY

EDWARD ELGAR.

(OP. 53, NO. 2.)

heart re-spon-sive swells, Then trem-bles in-to si-lence, in-to si-lence

heart re-spon-sive swells, Then trem-bles in-to si-lence, in-to si-lence

heart re-spon-sive swells, Then trem-bles in-to si-lence, in-to si-lence

heart re-spon-sive swells, Then, then . . trem-bles in-to si-lence as be-

as be-fore, in-to si-lence as be-fore.

as be-fore, in-to si-lence as be-fore.

as be-fore, in-to si-lence as be-fore.

-fore, in-to si-lence as be-fore.

Rome, Dec., 1907.

TO MY FRIEND W. G. MᶜNAUGHT, MUS. DOC.

O WILD WEST WIND!

PART-SONG FOR S.A.T.B.

THE WORDS WRITTEN BY SHELLEY

THE MUSIC COMPOSED BY

EDWARD ELGAR.

(OP. 53, No. 3.)

* With the greatest animation but without hurry.

Copyright, 1908, by Novello and Company, Limited.

24

26

Win - ter comes, ... can Spring be far, be far be -

Spring, can Spring be far be-hind, . . can . . Spring be . . far, be far be -

can Spring be far be-hind, if Win - ter comes, can Spring be far, be far be -

Spring be far, can Spring, can Spring be far, far be - hind, can

Win -ter comes, can Spring, can Spring be far, far be - hind, can

- hind, can Spring be far, . . can Spring be far be - hind?

- hind, can Spring be far, . . can Spring be far be - hind?

- hind, can Spring be far, . . can Spring be far be - hind?

Spring, can Spring be far, . . can Spring be far be - hind?

Spring, can Spring be far, . . can Spring be far be - hind?

Rome, Dec., 1907.

TO MY FRIEND PIETRO D'ALBA.

OWLS
(AN EPITAPH)
PART-SONG FOR S.A.T.B.
WRITTEN BY
EDWARD ELGAR.
(Op. 53, No. 4.)

All that can be is said. No - thing.

All that can be is said. No - thing.

All that can be is said. What is it?

All that can be is said. What is it?

No - thing; A wild thing hurt but mourns in the night,

No - thing; A wild thing hurt but mourns in the night,

What is that? A wild thing hurt but mourns in the night,

What is that? A wild thing hurt but mourns in the night,

Rome, Dec., 31, 1907.

THE CHORAL MUSIC OF EDWARD ELGAR

THE APOSTLES
Oratorio for SATBB soli, chorus & orchestra

CARACTACUS
Cantata for STBarB soli, chorus & orchestra

THE DREAM OF GERONTIUS
Oratorio for M-S TB soli, chorus & orchestra

THE EARLY PART SONGS (1890-1891)
For SATB with divisions

FIVE UNACCOMPANIED PART-SONGS opus 71, 72 & 73
For SATB with divisions

FOUR LATIN MOTETS
For SATB & organ

FOUR UNACCOMPANIED PART-SONGS opus 53
For SATB with divisions

FROM THE GREEK ANTHOLOGY
Five unaccompanied part-songs for TTBB

GIVE UNTO THE LORD (PSALM 29)
For chorus & orchestra

GREAT IS THE LORD
For SATB chorus & organ or orchestra

THE KINGDOM
Oratorio for SATB soli, chorus & orchestra

THE LATER PART-SONGS (1902-1925)
For unaccompanied SATB with divisions

THE LIGHT OF LIFE (LUX CHRISTI)
Oratorio for SATB soli, chorus & orchestra

THE MUSIC MAKERS
Ode for contralto solo, chorus & orchestra

SEVEN ANTHEMS
For SATB (one for SA)

THE SPIRIT OF ENGLAND
For S or T Solo, chorus & orchestra

TE DEUM & BENEDICTUS IN F
For SATB chorus, orchestra & organ

THREE UNACCOMPANIED PART-SONGS
For SATB with divisions

ISBN 0-85360-316-2

NOVELLO PUBLISHING LIMITED
14 - 15 Berners Street, London, W1T 3LJ
Exclusive distributors:
Music Sales Ltd.
Newmarket Road, Bury St. Edmunds, Suffolk, IP33 3YB

9 780853 603160

Order No. NOV072324R